Published by
Don Namor Press
Farnham

Sacred Stones and Holy Water
ISSN 1743-1778
I: Mother Ludlam's Hole
ISBN 0-9547172-0-1

©2004 Roman Ilmar Golicz

*First published April 2004
Reprinted with minor corrections June 2004*

Front cover:
Artist's impression of how Mother Ludlam's Hole
may have looked before the 13th century.
Acrylic ©2004 Miriam Golicz

Typesetting and design by Don Namor Press
Printed and bound in Great Britain by
Kall Kwik business design & print,
83 West Street, Farnham

The confused account, heavily abbreviated and written in three different hands with further interpolations, as it appears within the annals of Waverley Abbey describing how Brother Simon supposedly discovered Mother Ludlam's Hole

[British Library MS Cotton Vespasian XVI f.110v]

Brother Simon and the Waverley manuscript

Approximately 550 yards (500m) north-east of the ruins of Waverley Abbey, the first Cistercian foundation (1128) in England lying south-east of Farnham, is Mother Ludlam's Hole, a modest cave within Moor Park situated along the line of a ridge beside the River Wey. It is number 1712 in the official list of Surrey antiquities.

The monks of Waverley Abbey maintained a chronicle in which the history of their foundation was recorded, and under the year 1216 is an entry that appears to describe what happened to a local source of water and how the problem was solved:

Hoc anno non sine multorum admiratione exinatinus est fere omnio et exsiccatus fons lavatorii nostri videlicet Ludewell. Cujus ubertas per multorum curricula annorum diversis officinis in abbatia aquas largissimas profluo cursu ministraverat abundanter. Fonte igitur deficiente et per officinas more solito minime discurrente. Pro praedicti fontis inopia vehemens nimirum infra abbatiam oritur molestia. Hujus igitur infortunii incommoditatem quidam monachus ex nostrii frater S considerans et graviter ferens subtiliter coepit mente tractare animoque disponere qualiter praedicto incommodo posset citius et congruentius subvenire. Excogitato itaque consilio utili et tandem reperto accingens se fortiter aggressus est opus satis durum scilicet exquirere et indagare novas aquarum vivarum venas quibus cum magna difficultate inquisitas et inventis atque in unum non sine multo labore et sudore redacta industria sua coegit omnes easdem venas simul per quendam ductum subterraneum ad unum locum descendere et in eodem loco fontem vivum et perpetuum non natura sed arte conficere. Cujus perennis cursus sicut patet cernentibus praedictis officinis abbatiae aquarum copiam suam largitate utiliter subministrare non cessat. Vocabulum fontis est Sanctae Mariae fons.
Vena novi fontis ope Symonis in pede montis
fixa fluit jugiter fistula format iter

[This year, not without considerable astonishment, the spring – namely Ludewell – serving our *lavatorium* became almost dry and empty. This spring for many years running had served various abbatial functions with copious quantities of flowing water. So when the spring failed grave concern spread throughout the abbey. A certain brother of ours, Simon, disturbed by the prospect of this misfortune, applied his intelligence and considered how to remedy this problem. When he had at last conceived a plan, he tackled the matter; that is, he set out to explore and to find a new and lively source of water, which with great difficulty and much labour being found, he brought these sources together and at the same time caused an underground duct to be brought to one place, and to the same location was channelled a vigorous and continuous spring – accomplished by design rather than through natural fortune – whose continuous flow, as is plain to all, provides all the water required by the abbey. The name of the spring is Saint Mary's Spring.
The stream of a new spring well, Simon's opus at the foot of a hill,
flows in a ceaseless channel, the route by means of a tunnel].

The chronicle as it exists today, in a single manuscript, runs from the Incarnation to 1191 where it breaks off abruptly. The history of the manuscript is complex, but for the purpose of this monograph it is sufficient to establish that from 1201 to 1219 the entries were compiled retrospectively in 1219, while from 1219 to 1291 they are contemporaneous with the events described but in several hands. From 1158 the chronicle contains numerous marginal notes in a post-1219 hand. Thus the entry describing Brother Simon's activities *should* have been written in 1219, three years after the event. But it is clear that this entry was an even later insertion by two hands (line 7 *molestia* to *Hujus* marks the break) each of which was distinct from that of the 1219 compiler, with the two lines of verse squeezed into the tail of the parchment by yet a third hand. These crucial facts are never made clear by those translating the published transcript (Luard II 284-5). Perhaps this third insertion was Simon himself in a moment of twilight vanity since the monk in the principal heavily abbreviated entry was referred to simply as 'S' by scribal convention. At any rate, his is the only low-status contemporary name to come down to us from the entire chronicle.

Whosoever wrote and inserted the account, it is very confusing and misleading. The chronicle also tells us, briefly under the year 1179, of the completion of the *lavatorium* and provision of a source of water for it [*Hoc tempore lavatorium nostrum, et aquaeductus parata sunt* (Luard II 241). In this context, the word '*aquaeductus*' need not imply the common impression of an artificial aqueduct but simply the right or ability to convey water to a place]. This notice does not occur in the text but is one of the many marginal notes inserted by a later hand that again was not the 1219 compiler. What might all these curious interpolations mean?

The Cistercians planned their abbeys with great care, sending experienced teams to survey prospective sites before acquiring the land. In his *Journey Through Wales*, Gerald of Wales (1145-1223) stated that whenever the Cistercians settled in some wild and secluded retreat, within a couple of years they will have converted it into a fine monastic community with more wealth and land than can be imagined. This is exactly what happened at Waverley Abbey. The original grant of sixty acres in 1128 became 521 acres twenty years later, which included active farms and a working mill.

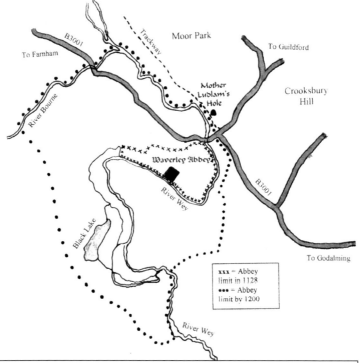

Plan of Waverley Abbey indicating the expansion of the monastic limit and the location of Mother Ludlam's Hole, which was never officially in the possession of the abbey

Why then was there apparently no water source before 1179? If Ludewelle indeed dates to that year, as a separate discovery, how did the surveyors miss it in the 1120s?

Were the monks using river water for half a century before stumbling onto a source of pure water? If Ludewelle, whatever its origins, ran dry in 1216 as the record seems to claim, why did Brother Simon simply not excavate the existing source rather than undertake the difficult and uncertain task of finding and creating a new site? If this could have been achieved in 1216, why did those trained to do so not do this in 1128? Where, in that case, is the 1179 source and the one that ran dry in 1216? This received interpretation of the chronicle is not even supported by the text, which names the two later water sources as both Ludewelle and Saint Mary in an act of careless repetition while also stating that the 1216 source became 'almost' and not completely dry.

Natural springs run dry either through prolonged aridity or internal collapse, and not in the way a cistern might when it empties. It is absurd to suggest that Brother Simon somehow located a new source and excavated several hundred feet into the sandstone rock when he could simply resurrect the failed spring. Common sense suggests that Ludewelle and Mother Ludlam's Hole were in fact one and the same, with the ancient Ludewelle not yet a third site but again the same one alluded to in 1179, the year in which the monks obtained the right to draw water from it freely. A major internal collapse of the ancient spring caused Brother Simon to enlarge both the existing opening and the fissure to make reliable the flow of water. He then piped this directly to the abbey to prevent further collapse through constant usage. Fragments of this piping have been uncovered during excavations.

Unfortunately, by doing this, Brother Simon also destroyed the natural aspect of the cave and also any pre-medieval artefacts that may have been deposited within it. This is a pity, as Mother Ludlam's Hole enjoyed a long pre-medieval life as a minor shrine to the *genius loci* of an important late Iron Age, or Celtic, tradition, to which the name 'Ludewelle' ultimately owes its origins, and therefore also 'Ludlam' and the spurious prefix 'Mother'. Disentangling the disputed and eccentric etymology of 'Ludlam' and its related forms is the trackway towards understanding the cave's real history.

'Loud' or 'Lludd'?

Within the work on the natural history and antiquities of Surrey initiated by John Aubrey (1626-97) is a derivation sent to the editor, the scholar and topographer Richard Rawlinson (1690-1755), in 1717. This suggested that the element *Lud* referred to a king of the South Saxons who took refuge in the cave after being worsted in battle [Aubrey iii 361-3]. A century later, the antiquary Owen Manning (1721-1801) and his continuator William Bray (1736-1832) repeated this etymology, which became popular for two centuries. *Hlude* was a known proper name, but it was rare and the only historical 'Lud' in British kingship was Ludecan, king of Mercia from 825-27, who is not known to have encroached on the 'South Saxon' kingdoms of Essex and Kent. The only materially unhistorical 'Lud' was the mythical King Lludd living at the time of the Roman invasion of Britain. He was the son of King Beli the Great from whom the island of Britain was taken by the emperor of Rome who invaded it following a dream in which he saw a vision of his future Celtic empress. The cave's association with a different aspect of 'King Lludd' will be discussed later.

It has also been suggested that the first element of Ludlam is a corruption of Middle English *lafdi* for 'lady', itself derived from Old English *hlafdige*, loaf-kneader, for the person who made the bread – a woman. This derivation is clearly intended to lead one to 'Lady Well' (Ludewelle) and was supported in error by some antiquarians who nonetheless correctly appreciated that the 1179 source, Ludewelle and St Mary's spring, and Mother Ludlam's Hole were one and the same.

Manning and Bray also suggested that *leode wella* meant 'public well', and a later derivation proposed that this form meant 'sheltered well', neither of which seems plausible. After all, which well was not public? They are all public, a common-sense fact reflected in the Irish folk-tale of *Fior Usga* in which a king illegally seals off a public well used by the poor only for it to burst forth when eventually opened up. The resulting gush of pent-up water floods his palace and the surrounding valley in an act of justifiable retribution for such a gross violation, creating the Lough of Cork.

The received view, established by the English Place-Name Society, is that 'Lud' in all its forms before running water is descriptive for 'Loud', in this case 'Loud Well', examples of which, it is claimed, may be found in Derbyshire, Northamptonshire, Somerset, and Wiltshire. Again, this simplistic explanation defies common sense. Were so many springs really so noisy and their users so unimaginative that they could do no better than such associative terminology? Besides, as any visitor to Mother Ludlam's Hole today will testify, the flow of water there is virtually silent. Worse still, this form of Anglocentric academicism ignores the possibility that an English topographical feature may pre-date the Anglo-Saxon period – a common prejudice lying at the heart of British toponymy. Astonishingly, the heritage trail notice-board recently erected in front of the cave states that this derivation is Celtic.

In pre-Christian belief, British (Celtic) springs were invariably associated with feminine divinities such as Brigid (Brideswell), Coventina (Carrawborough), and Sulis (Bath), who subsequently were either subsumed by female saints (St Bridget of Kildare) or reinvented as the Christian *Theotokos*. The 'sacred spring' thus became the 'holy well'. But this Christianisation did nothing to diminish the magical potency of springs, and their waters were considered most suitable for use in baptisms and other Christian rituals. The quantity and distribution of Ladysprings and Ladywells, and those sites rededicated to the Virgin Mary and other female saints, strongly suggests that later Anglo-Saxons assumed 'Lady' as the convenient association with the pre-existing Celtic element 'Lud' in most forms surviving in this context. This easy association was derived from the general Celtic or Romano-Celtic association between natural springs and water goddesses; but there was also a specific religious association, hinted at with the story of 'King Lud', that was entirely missed.

Recent structural history

Waverley Abbey was dissolved in 1536, before which we may suppose that the cave had remained largely as Brother Simon left it; that is, a roughly hewn opening with crude flooring for maintaining the piping to the abbey. Later descriptions reveal a very different cave. The Hon. John Byng, Viscount Ebrington (1742-1813), who visited Farnham on 24 August 1782, was informed by the landlord of a public house that Mother Ludlam's Hole 'was not worth seeing'. Being thus determined more than ever to see it, Byng found that it was 'paved, has several stone benches in it, and is by much the best place I ever saw for a cold collation on a summer's day: never was a place more adapted for quiet meditation' [Andrews i 73-5].

But when the Radical publicist William Cobbett (1762/3-1835) visited the cave in 1823, he deplored the changes that had taken place since visiting it as a young man:

The semicircular paling is gone; the basins, to catch the never-ceasing little stream, are gone; the iron cups, fastened by chains, for people to drink out of, are gone; the pavement all broken to pieces; the seats, for people to sit on, on both sides of the cave, torn up, and gone; the stream that ran down a clean paved channel, now making a dirty gutter; and the ground opposite ... [is] a poor, ragged-looking alder-coppice [Cobbett i 371].

Technically, Waverley Abbey never owned Ludewelle as it lay just outside Bishop Giffard's original grant of land and was not included in the subsequent extension. However, it is unlikely that they would have tolerated interference with their water supply. Thus it was only after 1536 that Ludewelle could slowly revert to its original designation as a place for healing and devotion. The writer Jonathan Swift (1667-1745), who was employed as Sir William Temple's secretary at Moor Park House, often used Mother Ludlam's Hole for writing. Although such accounts of its use as a meditative location are common, it is not known precisely when it was adapted to serve as a genteel version of pre-Christian spring worship. However, it is probable that this was done at the behest of Sir William Temple, the cultured statesman and author who purchased the estate near Farnham in 1686 and named it Moor Park. Initially for the benefit of himself and his guests, after his death in 1699 it acquired a wider patronage as its local fame spread. We may assume that during the century and a half between the dissolution of Waverley Abbey and the acquisition of Mother Ludlam's Hole by Sir William Temple the site gradually returned to nature, a larger version of how it had been before Brother Simon excavated it. The present stone archway, measuring 10 feet (3m) in height at the apex and 15 feet (4m 50cm) across at the base, is a relatively recent construction. When Edward Wedlake Brayley (1773-1854) visited the cave in the 1840s, he noted that it was accessed through 'a natural archway in the sand-stone rock' [Brayley v 291]. For centuries this arrangement was satisfactory; however, decades of natural decay, aided by the assaults of wilful despoilers in recent years, diminished the internal dimensions of the cave. Without the Victorian stone archway it would have collapsed long ago. When William Adams (1828-91) visited

Mother Ludlam's Hole as it is today, photographed facing east

Mother Ludlam's Hole a decade after Brayley, he noted that it extended 'some thirty or forty yards into the rock' [Adams 364-5]. This did not refer to the rear of the cave, of course, but to the fluted opening of the fissure at the rear which it was at that time possible to walk virtually upright as though entering a corridor in a small house.

Today, Mother Ludlam's Hole is altogether just a little over 30 feet (9m) in depth, but speliologists surveying the site in the 1940s and again in the 1960s revealed some astonishing results. In August 1961, members of the Wessex Cavers Club were able to progress 192 feet (57m 60cm) down the spring channel at the rear of the cave from where they measured the distance ahead to where the channel divides, which was found to be 210 feet (63m). These statistics alone undermine the claim that Brother Simon accomplished this Herculean task rather than making good an existing spring.

1761 engraving of Mother Ludlam's Hole showing its use as a miniature spa

Moreover, the August 1961 exploration found the way ultimately blocked by a fall that had taken place since the previous expedition of December 1960, illustrating just how readily the cave is liable to collapsing. Thus when the floor level had been lower and when it had been fitted out according to surviving descriptions, the cave would have given the appearance of a comfortable miniature spa.

Celtic Church-not-made-by-hands

The healing properties ascribed to Celtic wells were not only mystical but also medical and the associated beliefs were ancient even two millennia ago. When the Romans appropriated the ancient springs at Bath they found that they were unable to assimilate Sulis – the Celtic goddess of healing spring waters worshipped in caves along the Severn estuary – into their own *Minerva Medica*, as was their custom as invaders, because the local cult was far too vigorous to be suppressed. They were instead obliged to combine them to produce the compound deity Sulis-Minerva.

In this context, we may now return to King Lludd, but in his true guise as a figure of British mythology rather than of bogus Saxon history. His father Beli is the Celtic god related to the Mayday Eve festival of Beltane, Latinised as Belenus and identified with Apollo by the Romans. Lludd is also a (masculine) Celtic deity, synonymous with Nudd/Nuadu (Latinised as Nodens) and in one aspect represented by the solar disc, like Horus of Upper Egypt, and in another as a water god. Lludd is a healing god, associated with the curative and life-giving properties of the sun and water, and whose vast and complex fourth-century shrine at Lydney in Gloucestershire, the best known of its kind in Britain, has been excavated to reveal a natural spring.

These curative springs are maintained in a widespread tradition. Local examples in Surrey include St Mary's Well at Dunsfold and the 'Bon-spring' at Witley, both associated with the magical treatment of eye infections. The water at Mother Ludlam's Hole was certainly always of the highest quality. In 1810, it was described as 'a copious discharge of a pure, transparent water' [Manning and Bray iii 140], and again forty years later as 'transparent and pure' [Brayley v 291]. This author has drunk at the spring on several occasions with no adverse consequences. However, it must be pointed out that the water has not been officially tested, although in November1985 the quantity was carefully measured at 6.6 gallons (30L) a minute.

This curative tradition survived into the twentieth century. A letter to the *Farnham Herald* (2 August 1985) by an elderly woman explained that as a girl she had been taken to Mother Ludlam's Hole by her grandfather who bathed her eyes with the water to ensure good sight. So potent was the Celtic belief in this curative power that spring water was drunk from a human skull in Pembrokeshire until the 1900s. In the Scottish Highlands and Islands, the faithful would take the trouble to obtain the skull of a suicide and fill it with sacred well water as a cure for epilepsy. On the island of Lewis, the exhumed skull of an ancestor was required.

It should also be remembered that the drinking of running spring water in the days of cholera and lesser water-borne infections was preferable to scooping up a cup of dirty liquid from a pond or slow-moving river. This is something the Cistercians appreciated, even if they did not understand it in a scientific way, and why they always searched for, and found, natural springs for their foundations.

Ducks and fissures

Curiously, the extent of the spring channel within Mother Ludlam's Hole and the fact that it bifurcates – facts apparently unknown before the twentieth-century surveys – add credence to another legend associated with it. The antiquary Francis Grose (1731-91) seems to have been the first to print (1787) the well known story of the duck that waddled into the cave, swam up the spring channel, and emerged a few days later in Guildford, eight miles (12.75 km) away. The story was not new when Grose heard it, and it has often been repeated with variations. Visiting the cave during the 1850s, the Aldershot printer and publisher William Sheldrake (1816-85) stated that it:

may be penetrated about thirty or forty yards when a barrier of trellis-work stops further progress … tradition, however, here steps in to our aid, and informs us 'that a duck was once put in this place and came out at St Catherine's Hill, Guildford', a distance of about ten miles [Sheldrake 103].

The Aldershot photographer and professor of music Charles Stanley Hervé (1809-97) noted the story in the 1860s, by which time the duck's point of exit had been identified as a fissure on the side of St Catherine's Hill [Hervé 169]. More realistically perhaps, another version has it that the duck, minus its feathers, emerged at Crooksbury Hill, which lies only half a mile (800m) east of Mother Ludlam's Hole.

It has been pointed out that this story is generic and conforms to the Animal Through Trip motif associated with several deep caves. Indeed, it is preposterous as a wholly genuine incident for who would notice, let alone identify, a duck emerging from a hole in Guildford and link it with another that disappeared days earlier at Farnham? However, the story may well be factual in so far as a duck had been seen entering Mother Ludlam's Hole not to emerge while another quite unrelated duck had been seen emerging from a hole elsewhere – whether Guildford or Crooksbury Hill. The link may be specious, but the belief that underground springs form a network of veins is not. At Dozmary Pool on Bodmin Moor in Cornwall there is a similar legend in which a thorn bush thrown in the middle later appeared at Falmouth Harbour, 40 miles (64km) away. These stories are neither foolish nor obscurantist. Dozmary Pool appears at first glance to have no source, but it is in fact fed and drained by the St Neot River, now interrupted by Colliford Lake, a reservoir, which is a tributary of the

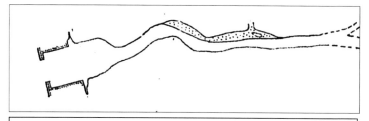

Speliological survey of Mother Ludlam's Hole conducted by the Wessex Cavers Club in 1961

Fowey. The thorn bush story explains the route of the water along these rivers out into St Austell Bay and then by tidal currents down to Falmouth Bay.

If such stories were intended to illustrate arcane geological and tidal knowledge the matter becomes more intriguing still in the light of the survey at Mother Ludlam's Hole, which revealed that the easterly channel does at least point in the direction of Crooksbury Hill and then, by extension, towards Guildford.

Sheldrake's mention of a trellis at the rear of the cave is confirmed by another account, also from the 1850s. This inner barrier was 'fastened very preventively over the farther opening of the cave, [and] saves from the influences of ... carbonic gas those adventurous spirits who fancy that they can find a road to Guildford by this path' [Young 147-8]. It appears that the internal fissure was once larger than it is today and people were able to walk almost upright some distance into it – without having to worry about carbonic acid gas, which this cave does not produce.

Sandstone is classed as a clastic arenaceous sedimentary rock; that is, it comprises sediments made up of fragments produced by the breaking-up of earlier rocks leaving a structure with grain sizes from one-sixteenth to two millimetres in diameter. Mother Ludlam's Hole is glauconitic, with green mica (a hydrous silicate of iron and potassium) as the cementing element, giving the cave its characteristic red, brown and yellow hues when it becomes oxidised on exposure to the atmosphere. Sandstone is insoluble but it is porous, and although it may be used as building material depending on the firmness of the cementing element, it is less durable than other types of stone. Certainly, then, the cave may have been reworked to bring together several veins, as the Waverley account suggests, with much subsequent remodelling; but it is highly unlikely to have been created in its entirety by Brother Simon or anybody else.

Inside Mother Ludlam's Hole today. Formerly, the floor level was considerably lower and the spring water flowed freely out onto the ancient trackway where it pooled

However, even more contentious than the question of who 'created' the cave and when is the issue surrounding the existence, or otherwise, of Mother Ludlam herself.

Mother Ludlam and her cauldron

Those who propose her to have been a real person living in the cave place her life to anywhere between the fifteenth and nineteenth centuries. An earlier date was preferred by Charles Hervé, supported by the *Surrey and Hants News* (4 July 1963) alluding to local folklore. Mrs Beatrice Anne Fry (1887-1974) claimed the later date (*Farnham Herald* 6 April 1973), stating that her great-grandmother, who had lived at nearby Stella Cottage in the 1840s, knew Mother Ludlam: 'She lived in a chamber of the cave just to the left of the entrance and she was a good witch'. Mother Ludlam supplied locals with herbal remedies and, having 'the gift', she was also able to locate lost property. Hervé's description of the flora around the cave in about 1860 certainly supports this notion: 'in it grew mosses, lichens, and fungi of species somewhat rare, whilst in its vicinity grew wild flowers, weeds, and medicinal plants in great abundance, forming ... a botanical garden' [Hervé 169].

There is no documentary evidence for Mother Ludlam at the cave (*cf.* the debate surrounding the identity of 'Black Annis/Anna' in her eponymous sandstone cave in the Dane Hills near Leicester). Thus Grose was forced to identify the cave as 'formerly the residence' of Mother Ludlam [Grose v 111], which is only the more elegant and scholarly way of opening a narrative with 'once upon a time'. In its issue of 2 October 1858, *The Illustrated London News* suggested with comparable vagueness that Mother Ludlam's Hole got its name 'from a tradition which assigns it as the residence of a white witch of that name'.

Mrs Fry's winsome picture of a benign *wicce* dispensing natural medicine and helping locals find their missing boots is a useful starting point, since most (but not all) accounts of Mother Ludlam portray her as an altruistic and utilitarian 'white witch'. Byng, in the passage already quoted, noted this interpretation as a legend already old in 1782: 'Mother Ludlam is reported to have been a witch of benevolent temper, who benefited, instead of injuring, her poor neighbours'.

Her most celebrated act of benevolence concerns the great cauldron now on display at Frensham parish church. It is of beaten copper measuring 2' 11" (87.5cm) in diameter and 1' 7" (47.5cm) in depth.

The story as it appears in the earliest known version, recorded by Aubrey in the summer of 1673, does not name Mother Ludlam's Hole. According to his local sources at Frensham, the cauldron originated in 'Borough-hill' in the tithing of Churt about one mile from its present location. That hill was inhabited by fairies who lent whatever item was required whenever the borrower knocked on a stone slab and asked for it, provided that it was returned either within a year or by a specified date. The cauldron was requested and given, but because it was not returned in time to be received by the fairies it had to be brought back to Frensham. For this breach of promise the fairies thereafter refused to lend anything again [Aubrey iii 366-7].

Aubrey's 'Borough-hill' has not been satisfactorily identified, but it may be either Bury Hill near Dorking or Borough Hill in Albury Park, while Mother Ludlam's Hole is about two miles (3.2 km) from Frensham. However, this need not disturb any investigator

'*Mother Ludlam's Cauldron*' *photographed by L. Wray 4 June 1910*

unduly. Mother Ludlam's Hole was, as will be shown, not so called in the mid-seventeenth-century when, as in Aubrey's work, it still appears as some variant of Ludewelle, while local estimates of distance in folklore are notoriously elastic. Moreover, although antiquaries continued to quote Aubrey, they had within a century grafted 'Borough-hill' onto Mother Ludlam's Hole, if indeed they were ever intended to be separate locations. Although this omission has implications for Mother Ludlam, it does not invalidate the belief in a connection between the cave and the cauldron.

Grose stated that Mother Ludlam was petitioned by the borrower arriving at her cave at midnight then turning three times around saying each time 'Pray, good mother Ludlam, lend me [item] and I shall return it within two days'. The requested item would be found in front of the cave the following morning, presumably at sunrise.

Nowhere after this date is the story ever divorced from Mother Ludlam. William Adams even went so far as to suggest that Aubrey had been mistaken and that 'Borough-hill' and Mother Ludlam's Hole were definitely one and the same location. Frensham also succumbed to this interpretation. The Reverend Dr John Charles Cox (1843-1919) was a Derbyshire historian, antiquary, and Radical publicist, but he spent ten years in Surrey and visited Frensham in about 1908 where he heard a story that painted a very different picture of Mother Ludlam to that recalled by Mrs Fry. After seeing the cauldron, he was informed by 'an old man hobbling along on two sticks' that Mother Ludlam was an evil witch used to 'brewing storms and every kind of evil by boiling up all manner of foul and filthy things' in the cauldron, which had been given to her as a present by the devil. It was a brave local parson who one day slipped into her cave, stole the cauldron, and placed it in Frensham church after washing it out in holy water. After that Mother Ludlam's power was destroyed [Cox 24].

London-born Eric Parker (1870-1955), who lived for many years near Godalming, also came across this nastier version of Mother Ludlam, and at about the same time as Cox, although he did not state precisely where or from whom he had obtained his information. In any event, he too heard that she had used the cauldron 'for boilings and philtremakings' [Parker *Highways* 32]. Forty years later, however, for the Surrey volume in the County Books Series, Parker did not mention Mother Ludlam or her eponymous cave at all.

Mrs Florence Stevens (1846-1937), who had been born in Castle Street and lived all her life in Farnham and Wrecclesham, deposited at the Museum of Farnham yet another version of the story culled from her manuscript memoirs written in the 1930s. According to what she had been told, Mother Ludlam was a beneficent wise-woman. One day, the devil appeared at her cave and asked for the loan of a large cauldron, presumably according to the correct procedure. However, as the devil spun around, his cloven hooves left their imprints on the ground, so Mother Ludlam naturally refused his request. Enraged, the devil stole the cauldron and bounded away, with Mother Ludlam chasing after him on her broomstick. At each of the devil's great leaps he left a mountain of soil, three of which are now known as The Devil's Jumps, two miles (3.2 km) south of Churt. But Mother Ludlam's broomstick was more than equal to the devil's leaps and she was forced to drop the cauldron onto one of his mounds, now known as Kettlebury Hill in the parish of Elstead. The disappeared into a hole now known as the Devil's Punchbowl, leaving Mother Ludlam free to collect her cauldron. She then deposited it at Frensham church for safekeeping.

All of these different versions have their own numerous variants. Mrs Fry accepted the basic cauldron story, but her great-grandmother had told her that Mother Ludlam, although a peaceful wise-woman, nevertheless cursed someone who had borrowed her cauldron and not returned it. According to Grose, she became angered by the lateness of its return and would not accept it, subsequently refusing to lend items again, much like Aubrey's fairies. Another tradition, clearly based on Mother Ludlam's earlier supposed date, has it that her cauldron was at first taken to Waverley Abbey and removed to Frensham in 1536 after the Dissolution.

What emerges from these stories is an engaging tangle of fairylore enmeshed in a ball of witchery dipped in treacle of myth. The fundamental element is that of the 'fairy loan', perhaps less common than 'borrowing fairies' but essentially the same story in reverse. A Scottish tale from Sandray in the Western Isles tells of a fairy who came to a herdsman's wife each day to borrow a kettle and return it filled with food. This exchanged depended on a rhyme that the wife was required to recite. When one day she was absent from home she entrusted this to her husband who, when the time came, refused to admit the fairy who then stole the kettle and did not return it. The wife was forced to go to the fairy hill to retrieve it.

Other conventional elements in these stories include the obvious association between witches and cauldrons, which in the popular imagination owes much to the caustic parody of the three witches in Shakespeare's *Macbeth*. The 'flying broomstick' recorded by Mrs Stevens owes more to Victorian fiction than to traditional witch-beliefs. The broomstick was first mentioned in English trial records for 1663, and although there are literary and symbolic precedents they rarely appear in official trial literature even after that date. The notion seems to have been derived from the psychoactive properties of some of the plants whose stalks were used to make broomsticks. Plants such as broomcorn, broomrape, and common broom were so used, as well as witch hazel. Broom (*Cytisus scoparius*) contains the toxic alkaloid cytisine that may have been used (along with many other psychoactive substances) to induce the sensation of flying among 'witches' who ingested it to aid their divinatory powers, as do the Yaqui magicians of Mexico today. Ironically, when the Christian priesthood sprinkled holy water with brushes made from common rue – another plant with strong witchcraft associations – they were employing miniature broomsticks.

However, it should not be assumed from all this that mundane explanations were never given. On the contrary, Aubrey only mentioned the Frensham legend in order to state his disbelief in it, reckoning instead that the cauldron belonged to the church and had been used for church-ale at parish feasts such as weddings and also for the relief of the poor at certain Christian festivals. The antiquary Nathaniel Salmon (1675-1742) agreed: 'The great Cauldron which lay in the Vestry beyond the Memory of Man was no more brought thither from Waverley than ... by the Fairies ... there having been many in England till very lately to be seen' [Salmon 139]. Salmon had probably seen the fine example at Lacock Abbey in Wiltshire, which dates to about 1500

There is also an important relic of Mother Ludlam's 'familiar' extant in the proverb most recently known in the form 'As lazy as Mother Ludlam's dog'. It seems that in true witch tradition, she had a close associate from the animal kingdom in the form of a black dog, albeit a not particularly effective one. As a guard dog it was virtually useless, as it had to 'lean against the wall [of the cave] to bark'. This item, which appeared in the *Farnham Herald* on 20 October 1983, gave evidence that the proverb was known as far away as Germany although it was at the time no longer used, or even much known, in Farnham.

These facts, and the proverb itself, provide the best clue yet for the existence or otherwise of Mother Ludlam while also providing a date for her name. The naturalist John Ray (1627-1705) recorded a close approximation in *A Collection of English Proverbs* (1670). It appears as the twenty-third entry under 'Proverbial Similies in which the Quality and Subject begin with the same Letter': 'As lazy as Ludlams [sic] dog, that lean't his head against a wall to bark'. This was the first collection of proverbs published in the English language. Ray, who began collecting in 1660, explained his method in his note 'To the Reader': 'I observed all that occurred in familiar discourse, and employed my friends and acquaintances in several parts of England in the like observation and enquiry, who afforded me large contributions'.

It may be wondered whether the Staffordshire poet Charles Cotton (1630-87) was one of Ray's 'friends and acquaintances'. In 1664, Cotton published *Scarronides*, a burlesque adaptation of Virgil's *Æneid*. In Book II, in which the Trojan prince Æneas relates the fall of Troy, he reclines so slothfully that Cotton likens him to 'Ludlam's curr, on truckle lolling'. In a marginal note, Cotton gives an explanation similar to the proverb shortly to be published by Ray.

So far, there was neither mention of 'Mother' Ludlam nor any reference to her cave in Surrey. In the second edition of Ray's collection (1768), the proverb's spelling was modernised but otherwise left as originally written. On 13 April 1850, a contributor to *Notes & Queries* declared that the proverb 'is so general and familiar in South Yorkshire (Sheffield especially) as to be frequently quoted' [1: i 382]. He reckoned that Ludlam was some obscure man, giving the proverb 'As lazy as Ludlam's dog, as laid him down to bark'. A number of subsequent contributors were unable to throw any light on the identity of Ludlam. However, the original writer recorded (15 June) that the mother of a Sheffield friend recently told him of a clearly degenerated legend involving '"the fat Miss Ludlam" ... a fat old maid and her fat poodle' [1: ii 43]. The poodle as we know it today was not known in Britain before the nineteenth century.

Ebeneezer Cobham Brewer (1810-97) in his *Dictionary of Phrase and Fable* (1870) recorded the proverb 'Lazy as Ludlam's dog, which leaned his head against the wall to bark' explaining that 'This Ludlam was the famous sorceress ... who lived in a cave ... She kept a dog, noted for its laziness, so that when the rustics came to consult the witch, it would hardly condescend to give notice of their approach, even with the ghost of a bark'. As a result of this, the matter was raised again in *Notes & Queries*. On 20 September 1873, a contributor confirmed that Ludlam was indeed 'the famous sorceress of Surrey' [4: xii 239]. In a letter dated 24 June 1954, the archaeologist and psychical researcher Tom Lethbridge (1901-70) was quoted a living Farnham source repeating that the dog '"Twas a lazy creature – so lazy that it had to lean against the wall of the cave when it wanted to bark"' [Oates & Wood 76]. The proverb could still be found in *Brewer's Myth and Legend* of 1992, and although it has disappeared from local usage, dog and witch are now inextricably bound together.

It is clear from this chronology that the association between Ludlam in what is obviously originally a northern proverb and Mother Ludlam from Surrey dates to the third quarter of the nineteenth century. The proverb may even be a simple variant of the Scottish proverb 'As lazy as David Lawrence's dog', where local dialect for laziness, 'larrence', has been corrupted to provide a specious human identity.

Nevertheless, there is a further interesting association here connected with Lludd as a healing deity. The Greek god of healing associated with Epidauros was Asklepios, son of Apollo, whose mother exposed him at birth to avoid the discovery of her pregnancy. Although the serpent became the sacred symbol of Asklepios, his mascot is the dog who protected and raised him after his exposure and who has been found depicted on votive objects at his shrine. Similarly, at the shrine to Lludd/Nuadu at Lydney, both votive objects carrying the image of a dog and dog sculptures have been unearthed, as have dog-cult finds at a number of Celtic caverns, shafts, and wells. This memory trace is probably responsible both for the existence of Mother Ludlam's 'familiar' and also the grafting of her name onto an old English proverb.

DESCRIPTION of Mother LUDLAM's HOLE, near FARNHAM, in SURREY.

MOTHER Ludlam's (or Ludloe's) Hole, as it is denominated, lies about half way down a fandy hill, towards the end of Moor Park, and three miles fouth of Farnham.

It is one of thofe caverns which the hand of Nature has hollowed out of the earth. The cavity at the entrance is nearly eight feet in height and 15 broad, decreafing till a perfon can only pafs through it on his hands and knees. The depth of it muft be confiderable; and farther on, after going through this narrow way, it is faid to heighten again, and it winds northerly at fome diftance from the entrance. It feems to have owed its formation chiefly to water, as there is a paffage at the bottom, which is paved, for a rill that runs through a fort of trough into a marble bafon, which has an iron ladle chained to it; and from hence it is carried out to the declivity of the hill by other troughs, and is collected into a fmall refervoir.

On each fide there are two benches placed for the conveniience of fuch as may chufe to meditate in this grotto.

According to tradition the place received its name from mother Ludlam, or Ludloe, a woman who feemed to take as much delight in doing good in her way, as the Weird Sifters were faid to do in the contrary practice. In particular, fhe ufed to fupply her neighbours wants by lending them fuch utenfils as they might ftand in need of. In effect, fhe appears to have borne the character of a White Witch. This loan was always obtained by reforting at midnight to the mouth of the cave, and after turning three times round, aloud repeating "Pray good mother Ludlam lend me (whatever the thing might be) and within two days it fhall be returned." Then the perfon going again early the next morning, found the thing requefted at the mouth of the cave.

It is eafy to conclude (if this were believed) that the place was not a little reforted to; and the old lady continued her kindnefs till a perfon that had borrowed a large cauldron, failed to return it at the time appointed. The White Witch was fo much provoked at this behaviour, that fhe would not take it back when it was left at the cavern; nor would fhe ever lend any thing afterwards. It is added, that the cauldron was carried to Waverley abbey in the neighbourhood, and at length depofited in Frenfham church, when that monaftery was diffolved.

Salmon (as a modern writer has obferved) mentions that there was fuch a cauldron in the veftry of the church juft mentioned, remarking at the fame time, " It was no more brought from Waverley than, as the report goes, by the fairies. It need not raife any man's wonder for what ufe it was, there having been many in England, till lately, as well as very large fpits to be feen, which were given for entertainment of the parifh at the wedding of poor maids; fo was, in fome places, a fum of money charged upon lands, and a houfe for them to dwell in for a year after marriage."

This may pretty well explain the latter part of the ftory. As to the reft, we only related it for the reader's entertainment; it will not bear a comment.

Sir William Temple, who fpent the latter part of his years at Moor Park in tranquillity, and whofe heart was inclofed in a filver box and buried under a fun dial in the adjoining garden, frequently ufed this as a place of meditation and retirement.

A typical eighteenth-century antiquarian description of Mother Ludlam s Hole. The stilted scholasticism of the Age of Enlightenment actually heralded a Dark Age for the study of British pre-history that survived until the Celtic revival of the mid-nineteenth-century

The onomastic devices employed by Mrs Stevens to explain away a number of local place-names were ingenious but not unique: the mounds and depressions in Britain's topography associated with the devil and his dominion over earthly matter are legion. Besides, there is another such explanation for the same topographical features, published in the *Farnham Herald* on 3 February 1950. In this, Thor [Thunar], the Norse god of thunder and lightning and killer of ice giants, was sleeping near Frensham when the devil came 'jumping around and woke him up'. Thor commanded him to leave, but the devil merely taunted him 'with being old and fat' whereupon the god 'picked up a huge stone and threw it hard and straight at his tormentor'. The devil fled across the hills, thus giving them their name, 'and on one of them, called Stony Jump, is the very stone which Thor had thrown'.

The manner of petitioning as noted by Grose also has precedents. At Pin Well in Alnwick Park, a celebrated wishing well, the supplicant must walk three times around it, throw in a pin, and only then make a wish. At the Scottish wells designated as curative for epilepsy, the patient must walk three times sunwise around them in order for the skull-water to have any effect. And then there is Mother Ludlam living in her cave in the first place. Caves were traditionally associated either with witch gatherings or as homes of individual witches such as the one at Wookey Hole near Wells in Somerset who, incidentally, also owned a dog. The 'witch' and prophetess Mother Shipton (Ursula Southiel, 1488-1561) may or may not have existed, but an alternative reading of her orthodox life is that she had been born in a Yorkshire cave where she lived for the rest of her days. Another association is found in the Arthurian story of Culhwch and Olwen, one of many Celtic stories by a people originally uninterested in written texts who developed instead a superlative oral tradition. In this, Arthur is set a number of tasks the last of which is to obtain the blood of the Black Witch of the North who lived in a cave. Cave-worship is a cult with its own history, but when combined with a natural spring the cave more than doubles its potency.

No account of Mother Ludlam and her eponymous cauldron may omit reference to the Egyptologist and folklorist Margaret Alice Murray (1863-1963). The cauldron was catapulted to international fame in 1931 when Murray included it in the second work of her trilogy dedicated to proving the existence of an aboriginal pan-European pagan witch-cult existing into the modern era. According to the material surrounding the brief mention of the cauldron, fairies were a memory trace of Early Bronze Age plain dwellers annihilated and demonised by Celtic invaders who subsequently transmuted their victims into fairylore [Murray 59]. It is some irony then that this is precisely what the Anglo-Saxons subsequently did to the Celts and are still doing today. However, the traditional theory that fairylore is a memory trace of ancient religious practices is more sustainable. It seems likely that Murray, who collected references to Mother Ludlam with the intention of eventually publishing a full study, was hoping to be able to establish Mother Ludlam as a genuine and active member of her theoretical witch-cult – perhaps even the leader of one of her alleged covens.

The inevitable conclusion is that Mother Ludlam, in her guise as a witch and holding that name, is a fiction. But it is a fiction with a difference. Mother Ludlam – as all cave witches – is a distorted relic of the Mother Goddess associated with Celtic springs and wells. In this interpretation the witch is pagan, harnessing the power of creation and nurturing with an obvious association between the cave and the womb of the Mother Goddess since Neolithic times, an association particularly obvious with burial chambers. Other deities born of cave-wombs were the West Asian celestial Mithra; the Phrygian god Attis; and even Christ in certain non-Western traditions. Merlin too, in one account, was born of a cave (near Tintagel in Cornwall) from which he saw and took King Arthur from out of the sea. At Mother Ludlam's Hole both male and female aspects are represented, with the setting sun streaming into the womb in the act of Sacred Marriage, a common theme in early spirituality.

During the sixteenth and seventeenth centuries, the prefix 'mother' was employed as a title for low-status women who had borne children. For these reasons, it acquired an increasingly pejorative sense, thus becoming associated with many 'witches' even beyond the period when this was fashionable. Thus Mother Agnes Waterhouse and Mother Eve of Hatfield Peverell (Chelmsford, 1566); Old Mother Stile of Windsor (1579), one of whose alleged victims travelled to Farnham to take advice of a local cunning man [Thomas 656]; Old Mother Alice Samuel (1513-93) of the Warboys Witches; Old [Mother] Demdike [Elizabeth Sowthern] and Old [Mother] Chattox [Ann Whittle] of the Pendle Witches (Lancashire, 1612); Mother Joan Flower of Lincoln (1618); and Mother Ruth Osborne of Tring (1751). The grafting of this tacitly derogative prefix to legendary or quasi-historical figures such as Mother Ludlam and Mother Shipton hardly required justification. It was a slow process. On the first Ordnance Survey map of the area, work conducted between 1792 and 1816, the cave is marked simply – and therefore more accurately – as 'Ludlam's Hole'.

There is even another local legend involving a similar character, known as 'Old Mother Squalls' of Aldershot, who is said to have lived in a small cottage by the banks of a tributary of the Wey, long since vanished. The epithet has been associated with such disparate figures as a midwife active in the 1670s, employed by the Vernon family of Farnham, to a wise-woman of the 1840s. This latter was a 'witch' who could 'plait the mane of a horse in an instant, curl a cow's tail, petrify a dog and send nervous animals scurrying into the nearby woods shaking in terror' [*Hampshire: the County Magazine* 20:7 (May 1980) 41]. The two stories have been collapsed to create a permanent 'ghost-witch' last reported 'seen' in 1971.

Herblore and healing are traditional crafts associated with the true *wicce* as an aspect of the Mother Goddess, while the so-called 'familiar' is the companion providing the *wicce* with a living link to the natural world. Old Mother Demdike (1532-1612) was also accused of having an evil familiar in the shape of a black dog, a harmless creature whose purpose had been perverted by the inquisitors of the day. The cauldron represents the fruitful belly of the goddess, and by tradition has always had three legs exactly like the Frensham example, which explains the association. When the cauldron is filled with water it may be used for scrying by observing images (*Hydromancy*), or the patterns made by molten wax (*Ceromancy*) or oil (*Leconomancy*) when these substances are introduced into the filled cauldron. Once demonised by the Church, this activity became Parker's 'boilings and philtremakings' so redolent of Shakespeare's loathsome witches.

But the association of Mother Ludlam and the cauldron is more profound and ancient than the perversions of later witch-beliefs. Magic cauldrons are common in British mythology and are for the most part healing vessels associated with gods and goddesses who function chiefly as healers. In the story of Taliesin, Ceridwen is the goddess of inspiration who brews up a magic potion in her cauldron to empower her deformed son, a potion stirred for a year and a day by the young Taliesin who accidentally ingests some of the liquid to become the bard of legend. The need to stir the cauldron for a year and a day represents an astronomical cycle, in the same way that the 'thrice sunwise' circumlocution at Mother Ludlam's Hole is a solar ritual representing duration of three whole days. Additionally, the figure of a circle has represented the solar disc and the male aspect (latterly Nuadu) since Neolithic times, as observed in megalithic spiral carvings chiefly in Ireland. The 'thrice sunwise' pattern may be derived from the Neolithic clockwise spiral motif symbolising the growing strength of the sun as it passes from winter to summer.

Another magic cauldron occurs in the story 'Branwen, daughter of Llyr'. In this literary myth, the cauldron is able to restore life to the deceased. It was owned by Llyr's brother Bran, king of Britain, who presented it to Matholwch, king of Ireland. Interestingly, Bran has been identified as Dicinius, or Delinus, who as Beli was the father of Lludd. It was this aspect of the cauldron as a healing vessel that gave rise to the legend of the Holy Grail as a large bowl, or dish, carrying the Salmon of Knowledge. This was converted into the chalice of the Christian Church containing the healing blood of Christ collected by his uncle Joseph of Arimathea, and also the baptismal font containing the symbolic waters of the River Jordan endowing the new life-in-Christ. That it was not vice-versa may be seen by the existence of such cauldrons in antiquity and recalling that Medea of Colchis was in possession of just such a device for reassembling and reanimating dismembered corpses. Once the Church had assimilated the curative properties of the healing cauldron as the communion chalice, the former healing vessel was demonised, as made explicit by the Frensham story of the priest cleansing it through 'baptism'.

Not 'Loud' but Lludd

As stated earlier, the Anglo-Saxon form for 'Lady' is the least ludicrous of the etymologies for the first element 'lud' proposed in the past. But in the general dismissive atmosphere surrounding sub-Roman British culture, scholars have chosen not to pursue the matter before the Anglo-Saxon period. 'Lud' is better derived from the Celtic healing deity Nuadu through the form 'Lludd'.

Prejudicial attitude has produced the received wisdom that Lydney, known as Lidaneg in a tenth-century Anglo-Saxon charter, derives from 'Lida's island' for no better reason than that a pre-Saxon-conquest origin has been ignored. Clearly, the toponym also derives from the sub-Roman cult of Lludd/Nuadu introduced from Ireland centuries before the Anglo-Saxon period. Although a late shrine dedicated to Nodens, Lydney is complex and may have been grafted onto an earlier cult along the banks of the River Severn. This cult is recorded as far away as London where a shrine gave rise to Ludgate, while the historicised myth states that King Lud gave his name to the entire settlement. The base element does derive from a personal noun, and a potent Celtic god known to have had an early shrine there is the logical answer. It is not known whether this cult spread from east to west or vice-versa, or whether it was prevalent among all the Celtic tribes. In any event, Mother Ludlam's Hole does lie comfortably on a line between the two, situated on a ridgeway with the customary ancient trackway associated with many such natural features.

Such a foundation legend, dressed up as early medieval Christian history to disguise its Celtic pagan origins, exists in the case of Ludgvan in south-west Cornwall. This legend states that an Irish missionary named Ludgvan (clearly the assimilation of the cult of Nuadu from Ireland) built the local church. In order to encourage the Christian devotion of the local population, Ludgvan prayed for a miracle whereupon a sacred spring welled up from the dry earth – a magical spring that improved his sight when he washed his eyes in the clear water and also improved his voice when he drank it. Ludgvan is now venerated as a local saint, but there was in fact no such man. The preposterous and entirely circular 'official' etymology of Ludgvan states that the church and village are named after 'Ludwan'. In reality, the foundation legend is as accurate an account of the cult of Nuadu latterly absorbed by Anglo-Norman Christian tradition as it is possible to conceive.

It is now generally accepted that Celtic was the common tongue of the British below the ruling elite right through the Roman period and remained so before the eradication of Celtic culture throughout England by the Anglo-Saxons. Ancient places retained their ancient names until their annihilation or transmutation following the Anglo-Saxon invasion. Thus it may tentatively be suggested that all place-elements based on 'Lud' represent this Celtic or perhaps even pre-Celtic and assimilated cult. Nearly all are presently located near water, or by a spring or well, and at one time all may have been so located. At Lydstep near Tenby in South Wales, for example, there is even a series of natural caverns open to the sea, just as Mother Ludlam's Hole faces its stream in a depression that often floods giving the impression of a deluged forest. This feature would have been more obvious before the digging out of the exterior channel with its supporting walls in the time of Sir William Temple and both the raising of the trackway and the deposition of sandstone before it.

Ludlam's second element is uncertain but may include a corruption of the first two parts of the god's familiar nickname Lludd Llaw Ereint ('Silver-handed') where they have been conjoined and given a close phonetic pronunciation. This is supported by the fact that in some early sources the cave is referred to as Ludlow's or Ludloe's Hole. However, the medieval name Ludewelle, without a second element, may indicate that the addition was inserted merely for euphony as it did not produce something like 'Lude[lame/loe]welle' as may have been expected. Thus Ludewelle had the original sense of 'well of Lud', as retained in Ludwell near Shaftesbury in Wiltshire. This is not yet another tiresome Saxon warrior or landowner conjured up by topographers taking the path of least resistance but the Celtic deity who probably even gave the rare name Hlude to European Saxons. The similarity with the Anglo-Saxon *lafdi* can now be seen as merely coincidental, but useful as this has ensured the survival of the ancient toponym. 'Mother Ludlam' as a distinct personage, however, is therefore an aspect of the universal feminine deity associated with the cave and its natural spring just as the Blessed Virgin Mary was for the Cistercian monks, the 'lady' of Ludewelle for their predecessors, and Lludd/Nuadu before that.

The continuity and importance of this association in Britain is made plain in Arthurian literature. One of the darker elements of this primal quasi-historical myth is the concept of the Waste Land. Superficially an environment devastated by pestilence and drought, at a deeper allegorical level it represents a culture severed from its spiritual traditions. In *From Ritual to Romance* (1920), Jessie Weston established the common view that since Arthur and the land were one both he and his kingdom wasted away through the betrayal of Sir Lancelot du Lac and Queen Guinevere. This was transferred onto celluloid with force and dignity in John Boorman's film *Excalibur* (1981). Earlier texts, however, placed this seminal injury at the court of the Fisher King, the keeper of the Grail, which deep wound necessitated the Grail quest.

But another version appears in the *Elucidation*, an anonymous prologue to one of the manuscripts of the twelfth-century *Le Conte del Graal*. In this, Arthur's kingdom becomes a wasteland when the goddesses of the sacred spring wells of Britain are raped and their chalices – healing cauldrons – stolen. The Knights of the Round Table are charged with retrieving the chalices and returning them to their respective springs, subsequently becoming the sworn guardians of the goddesses. Once this is accomplished, the waters flow once again and the land is restored to health.

Finally, it is important to recall and note the sources in which Mother Ludlam does not appear. The antiquary William Camden (1551-1623) published his monumental

Britannia in 1586, a complete topographical, historical, and legendary account of England expanded in 1607. Although Camden described Farnham town, the castle, and Waverley Abbey, he made no mention of either the cave or Mother Ludlam. It has already been noted that neither Aubrey nor Salmon mentioned her although both discuss Waverley Abbey. As stated, Aubrey undertook his tour of Surrey in the summer of 1673. However, he did not publish the result, leaving Rawlinson to do this after his death. Rawlinson undertook his own journey through Surrey in 1717; he did not mention Mother Ludlam. The reason for this is clear: she was the product of an early Georgian corruption of the Celtic water goddess and recent witchcraft history. She is both Nuadu in his Welsh form of Lludd and the Great Goddess as the 'Mother' witch that by the early eighteenth century was part of household knowledge at the conclusion of the 'Burning Times' that had judicially butchered many hundreds of innocent women and men. The cave itself was more-or-less 'dormant' between the Dissolution and its resurrection under Sir William Temple.

The first trellis, 1874-90, photographed by the Farnham motoring pioneer John Henry Knight in about 1880

The trellis-work

However, all this does not necessarily mean that a mortal never inhabited Mother Ludlam's Hole. But it is unlikely that anyone could have lived there while it was in use by the monks of Waverley Abbey (c.1130-1536) or after its conversion into a genteel spa in the eighteenth century until this fell into decay in the early 1800s. Moor Park was acquired by the civil engineer John Frederic La Trobe Bateman (1810-89) in 1858, and it was he who installed the archway and first trellis in March 1874. The superfluous inner trellis was also

The second trellis, 1890 to c.1950, photographed 22 May 1909 by John Nowks of the Croydon Camera Club

removed when the outer one was erected. There was a gate in this outer trellis but it was kept locked. It was replaced by a more elaborate version in 1890 by the new owner Sir William Rose, 2nd Baronet (1846-1902), which elicited this comment from Eric Parker: '[the cave is] barred and gated and spiked with iron, evidently a fit habitation, once upon a time, for a very witch-like old woman. The gates, or rather railings which do not open, must have been placed there many years ago, for no initials have been carved ... on the stone within' [Parker *Highways* 47-8]. However, Parker was wrong to state that the trellis did not open. This second trellis remained in place until about 1950 when it was detached by the owners of Ludlam's Gate (the property in whose garden the cave lies) and placed to one side. A temporary trellis was erected until 1969 when this was removed and the second trellis was donated to the Museum of Farnham. A barbed wire fence was erected in place of the temporary structure. Early in 2002, a third permanent trellis was erected after a bid in 1999 to obtain funds for the preservation of the cave as part of the local tourist heritage trail. Sadly, the cave had been damaged since the removal of the temporary trellis. In 1973, for example, the roof above the stone archway was dug out almost causing the cave to collapse while at the same time depositing the great quantity of sandstone into it that can still be seen and which makes walking around rather awkward. The barbed wire fence was removed following the vandalism. The third trellis is a close copy of the 1890 model and, like it, has a gate that is not easy to identify from a distance.

The third trellis, installed in 2002

William Foote

But Parker was correct to imply that this arrangement prevented habitation, and it is only between the early 1800s and the erection of the first trellis that someone could have inhabited the cave. Indeed, someone did as a matter of historical record, for Mrs Fry also revealed that her great-grandmother had known William Foote, the world-weary middle-aged man who arrived in Farnham from London one day in October 1839 and almost immediately moved into Mother Ludlam's Hole.

However, Foote did not have the medieval constitution necessary to be a successful hermit. When Mother Ludlam's Hole became too cold and damp for him that winter he found another, cosier, hole to live in nearby. This is now known as Father Foote's Cave and lies about 150 feet (45m) south-east of Mother Ludlam's Hole. It was not a spring – or even a true cave – but a short natural dry fissure that Foote smoothed down and enlarged in places to produce a tunnel varying in height from 2 feet (47cm) to 4' 5" (1.32m) and in width from 3' 6" (1.2m) to 10' 10" (3.25m).

Foote lived in his new home with a few books, a carpetbag, and some spare clothes. He was often seen in town, usually in The Unicorn, an eighteenth-century public house on East Street, now demolished. Little is known of Foote's past, but he became a local celebrity very quickly. The landlord of The Unicorn befriended Foote and commissioned a local artist to paint a portrait of him, which was done from life sketches but painted posthumously. This portrait hung in the saloon bar until 1902 when The Unicorn disappeared to become a bicycle shop; the portrait also disappeared, somewhat mysteriously, and it has not been seen since. However, it was described in *Notes & Queries* on 22 November 1856: 'The portrait represents a haggard face, with a grizzly beard and moustache. It needs not a Lavater [Johann Caspar Lavater (1741-1801), a pioneering physiognomist] to discover a tendency to insanity in its wild and melancholy expression' [2: ii 405].

Foote did not long survive the rigours of the eremitic life during a British winter. On 14 January 1840, he was found lying on the footpath below his cave and he died later that day in Farnham from the effects of exposure and malnutrition, having probably fallen down the steep climb to his new home after a happy hour or two with the landlord of The Unicorn. He used to be known as Father Foote, as it was

Inside Foote's Cave, a dry fissure partly excavated by the unfortunate misanthrope

immediately, but of course erroneously, believed that he was a religious hermit of some type. Sadly, like the analyser of his portrait, the Victoria County History was probably nearer the truth when it described him as a 'lunatic' [VHCS ii 593]. Foote was buried in St Andrew's churchyard, and with him began and ended the only historically verifiable occupant of Mother Ludlam's Hole.

It has been suggested that Father Foote's Cave may be the original 'Ludwell' used from 1179 and which ran dry in 1216, with Mother Ludlam's Hole entirely excavated by Brother Simon. While superficially elegant, there is much that militates against this theory. It is clear from the structure of the fissure that water did not course through it, or create it, as both its height above ground and its elevation would make it unlikely as an exit point for a natural spring. The pressure required would have created such a flow that across the centuries the sandstone hill would show clear evidence of this in the form of a channel both within the fissure and down the side of the hill.

But the most important evidence against this theory is that advanced throughout this monograph. If Father Foote's Cave had run dry, logically Brother Simon would have dug that out to the same extent that is alleged in the case of Mother Ludlam's Hole. There is no folklore, nomenclature, or literary evidence associated with this fissure before William Foote crawled into it and enlarged it, before which it may have resembled little more than an unusually spacious warren.

A place of power and dreaming

One last and controversial point on the contentious issue relating to the occupation of Mother Ludlam's Hole needs to be made, and it may be introduced by a modern ghost story told to the author by the percipient in 2003. A retired schoolteacher resident in Aldershot was a child of four in 1937 when, with her parents and five siblings, she visited Moor Park one Sunday where they enjoyed a picnic lunch in front of the cave. The percipient then saw what she interpreted as the figure of a cook pass from one side of the cave to the other: 'I knew it was a cook, because I'd seen pictures in comics, and they were always dressed like this, in white, with a tall white hat. The adult-sized figure emerged from the tiny branch of the cave to the right and moved unhurriedly to the matching branch at the left, and disappeared into it'.

This testimony is interesting because the percipient recalled 'some sort of barrier across the entrance ... but certainly it didn't keep anybody out ... it was usually open, at least in the middle'. It is a pity that Eric Parker, when he issued the second 'revised' edition of his book, continued to maintain that the second trellis did not open at a time when a little girl was freely passing through it.

The existence in 1937 of the two side niches, whose purpose is unknown, undermines the widespread view that they were dug out by vandals after 1969. The fact that the 'cook' passed silently and slowly from out of one and into the other is of great significance for the cave, around which a number of current local legends have evolved. These fissures may be seen as the points of emission and absorption of a subtle geophysical phenomenon associated with ancient sacred sites currently receiving serious attention by researchers in numerous diverse fields.

'Incubation', or 'temple sleeping', in which worshippers slept at sacred sites conducive to powerful dreaming for the purposes of divination or even healing, or perhaps experiencing death-to-rebirth rituals, is a controversial aspect of such sites, but one not easily denied. Indeed, the temple of Nodens/Lludd/Nuadu at Lydney contains a number of stone beds now thought to represent such sleeping areas. Comparisons may be made with the series of caverns near Worksop known as the

Creswell Crags (in particular the one known as Mother Grundy's Parlour) and Old Hannah's Hole near Wetton, all in the Peak District and all facing a source of water. These caverns show clear signs of habitation since the Neolithic period, and in 1899 two walkers experienced a powerful electrical discharge from Old Hannah's Hole that shot across the valley below. Nearby is Thor's Cave, which seems to have acquired its name from the Norse god due to similar local associations with thunder and lightning.

Why certain locations might stimulate lucid dreaming is a debate outside the scope of this study, but possibly Mother Ludlam's Hole had a reputation for influencing either sleepers or long-term sitters and thus helped to acquire for it a strong tradition of habitation. As stated earlier, Jonathan Swift found it conducive to literary inspiration, composing his satire *A Tale of a Tub* (1704) inside the cave. In this context, it is interesting to recall that Mrs Beatrice Fry's 'good witch' lived in the left-hand niche into which the perceived 'cook' disappeared in 1937. Of course, it would have been hardly possible to actually live in this restricted space. Perhaps this story is also a memory trace of that geophysical phenomenon affecting perception through electro-magnetic field distortion of temporal lobe processes, the systematised theory now gaining currency as the explanation for localised 'paranormal' phenomena associated with certain natural topographical features.

The influence of this ancient site has affected local perception of it to an extraordinary degree. Unsubstantiated stories of 'fairy lights' (now often interpreted as UFO-related phenomena) and 'strange noises' are frequently told. When Mr Bateman installed the first trellis it was to a general outcry from the local population, who saw it as their right to visit the cave freely. Similarly, when there was a move in 1897 by Sir William Rose to close the ancient public right of way there were protests bordering on the riotous, principally because such a closure would deny them future access to the cave. In 1948 there were moves to demolish both Moor Park House and Stella Cottage, and possibly it was this that caused the second trellis to be removed for its safety, although the precise reason for this removal is still a mystery. In any event, each trellis, whether permanent or temporary, has suffered vandalism by those who feel drawn to enter Mother Ludlam's Hole and this is unlikely to change. The need to protect the site from the spiritually dead does not outweigh the need for free access, and the third trellis has already been forced open on at least one occasion.

Lily Lade and bats

The potency of the site is evident in the curious story printed for the first time by Charles Hervé. During the reign of William III (1689-1702), the Reverend James Lade of St Michael's Church, Aldershot, received a letter stating that his sister-in-law had died in Harwich leaving a baby, and that he was now the sole living relative and should claim it. It turned out that the sister-in-law was the daughter of an earl and she had refused to marry the nobleman selected for her and had instead eloped with an impecunious officer of a foot regiment – the Reverend Lade's brother. This man had then been executed on a false charge of treason. The baby was brought to London by Lade and presented to the earl in the hope that he would relent and accept responsibility. Instead, both vicar and baby were ejected with a curse from the earl that if he were ever to set eyes on his granddaughter again he should be stricken blind.

Sixteen years passed and the orphaned girl – baptised Lillian by her new protector – grew into a fine young woman. One day, the Reverend Lade and Lillian accompanied two young men – Lionel Fitzgibbon and Walter Harewood – on a botanical ramble in Moor Park. A sudden thunderstorm obliged the reluctant party to seek shelter in

Mother Ludlam's Hole, and while there a second party entered, they also having been taken by surprise by the storm. This second group included Sir William Temple and Jonathan Swift as well as the earl, who of course did not recognise his granddaughter. Once again, the Reverend Lade attempted to introduce the earl to Lillian, and once again the earl bellowed out his curse as he turned away. Just at this moment, a blinding flash filled the cave, and when it was over the earl was found insensible on the floor, having been struck by lightning and blinded.

Five years later, Lillian Lade was married to Walter Harewood. The earl, transformed by his experience, attempted reconciliation, but now his granddaughter rejected him. After several failed attempts, the earl at last succeeded in passing on to her a gift of ten thousand pounds after the wedding ceremony, which the couple accepted. The earl's former transgressions were then forgiven.

The story is generic and in its present form hardly likely to be an accurate telling of a historical event. Nevertheless, Hervé called this story 'Lily Lade: a legend of Mother Ludlam's Hole', stating that 'Lily Lade is also no creation of the fancy, but a real personage, and the chief incidents of her career *perfectly true*, with the substitution of ideal for real names, and the alteration of a few dates [Hervé 150]. The earl was given the absurd title of 'Knuckledown' when this would have been appreciated as based on the slang for both 'penniless' and a 'pickpocket'. The form of the story is a literary convention.

More important, however, is the inclusion of Mother Ludlam's Hole, as the entire story hinges on the use of a location that, according to this version, people loathed to enter on account of its terrible associations. The divine retribution the earl suffers as a result of a curse of his own making is also derivative. But whereas most such motifs involve Christian locations (for example, the popular and often comical variant in which a priest is struck by lightning in his own pulpit during a fire-and-brimstone sermon) here we have a case of a pagan divinity supplying the *deus ex machina* that propels the plot to its sugary – and certainly Victorian – conclusion.

The cave has encouraged an atmosphere of gothic gloom by also providing a home for several species of bat, particularly after the erection of the first trellis. Three have been identified in recent years, all evening bats (*Vespertilionidae*): Natterer's, or red-grey bat (*Myotis nattereri*); Daubenton's, or water bat (*Myotis daubentoni*); and the Brown Long-eared bat (*Plecotus auritus*). In the summer months these can be seen hanging from the protruding stone work of the Victorian roofing. Formerly, however, the cave was also home to the Greater Horseshoe Bat (*Rhinolophus ferrumequinum*), but this species declined in numbers to such an extent during the second half of the twentieth century that it is now virtually extinct, although it appears to be making a recovery in the south west of England.

The last word on Mother Ludlam's Hole belongs to the topographer Thomas Allen (1803-33) who visited it in 1830 and contradicted Cobbett's description quoted earlier. Allen stated that the 'bottom is paved' and not broken into pieces, carefully noting the 'two stone benches' that Cobbett claimed had gone. Perhaps the obstinate middle-aged social reformer and political commentator was inclined to exaggerate in one direction while the romantic destined to die young from the pan-European cholera epidemic was inclined to exaggerate in another. However, Allen ended his description of the 'remarkable cavern' with a sensitive eulogy that would be difficult to surpass:

The gloomy and uncertain depth of the receding grotto, the gentle murmur of the rill, and the beauty of the prospect seen through the dark arched entrance, shagged with weeds, and the roots of trees, seem to conspire to excite solemn contemplation, and to fill the soul with a rapturous admiration of the great Creator [Allen ii 234].

Bibliography

This bibliography contains all the works cited in the text in addition to those used for the writing of this monograph. All publications were issued in London unless otherwise stated.

Adair, John, *The Pilgrims' Way* (1978)
Adams, William Henry Davenport, *Black's Guide to the History, Antiquities, and Topography of the County of Surrey* (1861)
Allen, Thomas, *A History of the County of Surrey*, 2 vols (1831)
Andrews, Cyril Bruyn *The Torrington Diaries, containing the tours through England and Wales of the Hon. John Byng*, 4 vols (1934-38)
Aubrey, John, *The Natural History and Antiquities of the County of Surrey*, 5 vols (Dorking, 1975)
Barber, Richard, *The Holy Grail* (2004)
Baring, Anne and Jules Cashford, *The Myth of the Goddess* (1991)
Brakspear, [Sir] Harold, *Waverley Abbey* (Guildford, 1905)
Bord, Janet and Colin, *Sacred Waters: holy wells and water lore in Britain and Ireland* (1985)
Brayley, Edward Wedlake, *A Topographical History of Surrey*, 5 vols (1850)
Briggs, Katharine, *A Dictionary of Fairies* (1976)
Camden, William, *Britannia* (6th ed. 1607); trans. Philemon Holland (1610).
Cobbett, William, *Rural Rides*, 2 vols (1893)
Cox, J. Charles, *Rambles in Surrey* (1910)
Crossley-Holland, Kevin, *Folk-tales of the British Isles* (1985)
Devereux, Paul, *Earth Lights* (1982)
— *Earth Lights Revelation* (1989)
— *Places of Power* (1990)
— *Earth Memory* (1991)
— *Haunted Land: Investigations into Ancient Mysteries and Modern Day Phenomena* (2001)
Ekwall, Eilert, *The Concise Oxford Dictionary of English Place-Names* (Oxford, 4th ed. 1960)
Eliade, Mircea, *A History of Religious Ideas. Volume 1: From the Stone Age to the Eleusinian Mysteries* (Chicago, 1978)
Fells, Richard, *Underground Britain: Caves, Caverns, Mines, Tunnels, Grottoes* (Exeter, 1989)
Gimbutas, Marija, *The Goddesses and Gods of Old Europe 6500-3500BC: Myths and Cult Images* (2nd ed.1982)
— *The Language of the Goddess* (1989)
Gover, J.E.B., with A. Mawer and Frank Stenton, *The Place-Names of Surrey EPNS XI* (Cambridge, 1934)
Grose, Francis, *The Antiquities of England and Wales*, 6 vols (1773-87)
Hayman, Richard, *Riddles in Stone: Myths, Archaeology and the Ancient Britons* (1997)
Hervé, Charles Stanley, *Traditions about Aldershot* (Aldershot, 1865)
Hope, Robert Charles, *The Legendary Lore of the Holy Wells of England, including rivers, lakes, fountains and springs* (1893)
Hunt, Robert, *Popular Romances of the West of England; or the Drolls, Traditions, and Superstitions of Old Cornwall* (3rd ed. 1881)
Jacobs, Joseph, *English Fairy Tales* (1890)

— *More English Fairy Tales* (1894)
Jones, Francis, *The Holy Wells of Wales* (Cardiff, 1954)
Lacy, Norris (ed.), *The Arthurian Encyclopedia* (1986)
Luard, Henry Richards (ed.), *Annales Monastici*, 5 vols (1864-69)
Mackinlay, James Murray, *Folklore of Scottish Lochs & Springs* (Glasgow, 1893)
Manning, Elfrida, *Saxon Farnham* (Chichester, 1970)
Manning, Owen and William Bray, *The History and Antiquities of the County of Surrey*, 3 vols (1804-14)
Matthews, John and Caitlin, *The Aquarian Guide to British & Irish Mythology* (1988)
McLeish, Kenneth, *Myths & Folkstories of Britain & Ireland* (1986)
Meaden, George, *The Goddess of the Stones: The language of the Megaliths* (1991)
Melville, Richard and Edward Freshney, *British Regional Geology: The Hampshire Basin and adjoining areas* (4th ed. 1982)
Mitchell, Bruce, *An Invitation to Old English & Anglo-Saxon England* (1995)
Monaghan, Patricia, *The Book of Goddesses and Heroines* (St Paul MN, 2nd ed. 1990)
Murray, Margaret, *The God of the Witches* (1931)
Myers, J.N.L., *The English Settlements* (Oxford, 1986)
Oates, Caroline and Juliette Woods, *A Coven of Scholars: Margaret Murray and her Working Methods* (1998)
Parker, Eric, *Highways & Byways in Surrey* (1909)
— *Surrey* (1947)
Pollack, Rachel, *The Body of the Goddess: Sacred Wisdom in Myth, Landscape and Culture* (1996)
Rätsch, Christian, *The Dictionary of Sacred and Magical Plants* (Bridport, 1992)
Ray, John, *A Collection of English Proverbs* (1670; 2nd ed. 1768)
Robbins, Rossell Hope, *Encyclopaedia of Witchcraft and Demonology* (1959)
Ross, Anne, *Pagan Celtic Britain: Studies in Iconography* (1967)
— *The Folklore of the Scottish Highlands* (1976)
Salmon, Nathaniel, *Antiquities of Surrey collected from the most ancient Records with some Account of the present State and Natural History of the County* (1736)
Salway, Peter, *Roman Britain* (Oxford, 1981)
Senior, Michael, *Myths of Britain* (1979)
Sheldrake, William, *Guide to Aldershot and its Neighbourhood* (Aldershot, 1859)
Simpson, Jacqueline & Steve Roud, *A Dictionary of English Folklore* (Oxford, 2000)
Smith, Albert Hugh, *English Place-Name Elements*, 2 vols (Cambridge, 1956)
Stenton, Sir Frank, *Anglo-Saxon England* (Oxford, 3rd ed. 1971)
Swanton, Michael, *The Anglo-Saxon Chronicles* (1996)
Thiselton Dyer, Thomas Firminger, *The Folk-Lore of Plants* (1889)
Thomas, [Sir] Keith, *Religion and the Decline of Magic* (1971)
Thorpe, Lewis (ed.), *Gerald of Wales: The Journey through Wales / The Description of Wales* (1978)
Tobin, Stephen, *The Cistercians: Monks and Monasteries of Europe* (1995)
VHCS, *Victoria History of the County of Surrey*, 5 vols (1902-12)
Vickery, Roy, *A Dictionary of Plant Lore* (Oxford, 1995)
Watts, Victor, *The Cambridge Dictionary of English Place-Names* (Cambridge, 2004)
Westwood, Jennifer, *Albion: A Guide to Legendary Britain* (1985)
Wheeler, Sir Robert Eric Mortimer & Lady Tessa Verney Wheeler, *Report on the Excavation of the Prehistoric, Roman, and Post-Roman Site in Lydney Park* (1932)
White, Richard, *King Arthur in Legend and History* (1997)
Young, Marianne, *Aldershot and All About It* (1858)